Marina & Ruby

Training a Filly
with Love
by Patricia Sayer Fusco and Marina Fusco
Photographs by Paul Fusco

William Morrow and Company, Inc.
New York 1977

We wish to thank those people who
helped to make this book possible:
Anthony Fusco, son and brother; Eric
Sharpnack, D.V.M.; Carrie McFadden,
horsewoman; Dan Argraves, farrier; Jeri
Spowers and Melinda Rosenthal; and
Robert Winkelmann, owner of the
ranch by the sea.

The C.S. Lewis quotation is used with
the permission of the Macmillan
Publishing Company, Inc., and The
Bodley Head, Ltd.
The Last Battle, by C.S. Lewis
© Macmillan Publishing Company, Inc.
The Last Battle, by C.S. Lewis
published by The Bodley Head.

Designed by Will Hopkins

Printed in the United States of America.

1 2 3 4 5 6 7 8 9 10

Library of Congress Catalog Card
Number 77-80233

ISBN 0-688-03229-X

Library of Congress Cataloging in
Publication Data

Fusco, Patricia Sayer.
  Marina and Ruby.

  Bibliography: p.
  SUMMARY: Pictures and text
record a girl's raising her horse to
maturity. Includes information on
training and health care.
  1. Horses—Juvenile literature.
[1. Horses] I. Fusco, Marina, joint
author. II. Fusco, Paul. III. Title.
SF302.F87   636.1   77-80233
ISBN 0-688-03229-X

Contents

Introduction

The story of this book began with a dream. Our daughter, Marina, was the dreamer, a girl who lived in Manhattan, where the only horses she saw were those of the mounted policemen in the park and the rental horses of the fashionably dressed riders on the city's bridle paths. But she had a vision of herself riding freely over hills and through forests.

She drew and painted pictures of horses, read books about them, and collected plastic statues of horses by the dozen.

We left Manhattan for two summers and lived in a tiny seaside village in California, where Marina's dream began to come true. Each day she went out with an older girl who was an experienced rider and a good teacher. They rode through the golden grass of the mesa, through tunnels of eucalyptus trees and down to the beach, where her mount liked to play in the surf.

The horse she rode was named Trixie—a sturdy, gentle but independent Welsh mountain pony, just the right size for a young girl. Each September, Marina returned to New York to remember those rides and to dream of owning her own horse.

The next summer, our family moved to California for good. During our first year there, a wonderful thing happened: Trixie's owner was forced to sell her when she moved away. As a surprise for her twelfth birthday, Marina became the owner of the horse she loved.

That was a beautiful time. Marina rode with her friends on the trails winding around the foothills and over the mountain near our town. They went on a long cross-country trek, camping overnight in the redwood forest.

Now another dream began to stir. Marina wanted to breed Trixie, to have a foal she could raise from the moment of birth.

Her campaign to convince us began in earnest. She read books, talked to owners who had bred their horses, and even called stud farms to find out what expenses were involved. Finally, she won us over. Trixie was no longer a real challenge for Marina, who by then was a more advanced rider, and we all knew that the mare would be a good mother.

So it was settled. Our veterinarian examined Trixie and when the time was right, we put her into a trailer and took her to the stud farm. There the perfect stallion waited: S.J. Serjet, a dappled silver Arab who was just the right size—and whose lineage was impeccable.

Then began a long, long wait for Marina: eleven months of dreaming and planning, waiting for the day the foal would be born. She followed Trixie's progress carefully, giving her the proper feed and extra vitamins, and not riding her once the pregnancy was advanced. The first time she felt the foal move inside the mother's body, Marina was ecstatic. As the time approached for Trixie's foaling, Marina checked her each day for signs of pre-labor.

At the ranch where she was stabled, Trixie was put into a separate corral, away from the other horses, to await the birth. And then the dream came true at last.

This book tells the story, in pictures and words, of two years of love and work and training, from that birth until the time when Marina could ride her own horse—freely, over hills and through forests.

—Patricia Sayer Fusco

9

A Whole World Waiting

The call from the ranch manager came early one August morning, just as the fog was beginning to lift. Trixie, like most horses and true to her own independent spirit, had foaled during the night, and Marina had missed the experience of watching the birth.

Her brief disappointment changed to high excitement as she rushed to the ranch. She flew across the ground toward the fenced-in field bordered by tall trees. There she found Trixie, casually munching hay, and a little filly, dark and still awkwardly new to the world. Marina froze, silent for a moment, seeing for the first time this small creature, so delicate and finely wrought.

She slowly approached—on her knees, because the foal was lying down—and touched her carefully. She made sure that all was well, feeling that warm body beneath the soft coat. The earth where the filly lay was still damp from her birth.

From that very first touching, there was no fear, no distrust. Even when she looked to her mother, who was still munching, the foal remained with Marina and seemed to recognize that she belonged there.

It was a gentle introduction. Though some mares become possessive about their foals, Trixie trusted Marina with her baby. The filly was certainly curious as she was caressed, but she seemed content to allow this soft intrusion into her new life—for a while. Then she was up on her feet, ready for some nourishment of her own.

Marina watched closely to see that the nursing went well. During the first few days after foaling, the mare's milk is actually colostrum, richer than ordinary milk. It contains extra protein and Vitamin A, as well as antibodies which protect the foal against certain infections, and has a laxative effect. As the filly nursed, Marina checked to make sure she had a proper hold on her mother's teat. When there was a pause in the nursing, Marina touched her again to reassure her and to reestablish the connection between them.

The sooner a foal becomes accustomed to human touch, the better. When the foal moved, following her mother for the first time, Marina was right there with her. When they stopped, she held her with hands firmly but gently cradling her chest, to let her know there was no reason to run away, that she would not be harmed. Quiet hands and a soft voice were the elements of that very first control on Marina's part—a gentle forcefulness.

It was amazing to watch a newborn animal become so quickly, energetically active, running and exploring. In their wild state, mares and foals must be prepared to join the herd and keep up with them as soon as possible after the birth; the same adaptability exists in domesticated animals.

Marina had spent weeks trying to find ideal names, both male and female, and checking to see that they were not already listed in the registry of the International Arabian Horse Association.

The name she had chosen for a filly, at the suggestion of a friend, was Miss Ruby Tuesday. It seemed to fit the dark little foal with one white sock. Ruby was a *fine* name for her.

Ruby was already very curious. Marina knew she had to do something about the fence around the corral. It was not filly-proof, since it had spaces high enough off the ground for Ruby to slip through. One of Marina's first tasks was putting up some extra lengths of fencing, with her father's help, to keep her horse safely where she belonged.

It was hard for Marina to leave the ranch that morning, even for a celebration breakfast. The reality of Ruby's new life was so exciting, such a miracle.

But she knew that the horses needed quiet and rest. And she had to call the veterinarian, who would check the mother and the filly to see that they were in the best of health, and give Ruby her first inoculations. She also had to call her friends, to announce Ruby's arrival!

She took one last long look at Ruby, who was sleeping peacefully in the corral. In the eucalyptus-scented air of that August morning, their life together had begun.

From then on, Marina's activities were focused each day on the ranch. She could hardly wait to see Ruby, to know that all was well. She spent hours there, playing and running with the filly, touching her and talking quietly to her.

Marina had strong ideas about the way she wanted to raise her horse. She had raised other pets and had lived with Trixie long enough to know the importance of a relationship based on closeness and trust. She had seen what happened when people mistreated their horses and withheld affection: the results were fear and confusion.

Animals treated with love and good feeling become not just *well-trained* but well-adjusted creatures who learn new things easily because they trust their trainers.

On the other hand, Marina did not intend to spoil Ruby. She meant to maintain an attitude of gentleness toward her, rewarding her with affection immediately when things went well, and being firm—not harsh—when corrections were necessary. This was her plan, and she used it from the very outset of their work together.

The postnatal care of both Trixie and Ruby was crucial. Newborns are especially susceptible to digestive troubles; even though Ruby had been inoculated, it was important to make sure that she did not develop constipation or scour (diarrhea). Trixie was given a good supply of tepid water, and her food was adjusted from a grain-free ration at the time of foaling to her normal diet three days afterward. During the first month, the grain ration was gradually increased to strengthen her and to augment her milk supply.

At the same time, Ruby, who seemed to find her mother's feed tasty, was given a special feed of bran meal to supplement her diet of milk.

Some horse trainers halter-break a foal several hours after birth, and all experts agree that this should be done within the first couple of weeks, while the animal is still small enough to hold.

Using a halter, one can apply gentle pressure to the horse's head. This is the first restraint employed to teach the horse that it may be controlled. The pressure does not cause pain; it is a reminder that the trainer is in command, and the close contact helps teach the horse to respond.

When Ruby was a week old, Marina brought her a soft, fuzzy foal halter. Ruby experienced for the first time the physical control which would be the basis of all her training.

Marina enticed her into a corner with a handful of her feed. Then she gently slipped the red halter over her muzzle, standing behind Ruby with her knee up to hold her. Ruby stood still for this, but she put her ears back in a show of disapproval. When Marina began leading her for the first time the filly balked at the new sensation. The earlier work did pay off, though: she calmed down when Marina placed a firm hand over her rump, and became still when she put her hands on Ruby's neck to steady her. It was the first big step.

Marina celebrated with a ride on Trixie—the first since the month before she foaled. It was a wonderful feeling, being on her horse again—even for a short turn around the corral—with the filly watching!

Marina also worked at helping Ruby feel comfortable when her feet and legs were touched. She quickly learned to stand quietly when Marina lifted a foot for inspection. It was an important lesson, since the inspection and care of the hooves by rider and farrier are constantly necessary.

During those first months, Marina rode Trixie in the corral and Ruby frisked alongside, growing stronger every day. The time had come for the next stage: leaving the corral for the first time.

Marina opened the gate and rode Trixie a few feet beyond while Ruby stood inside, puzzled at the new development. She watched as they moved away, but she remained firmly planted on her side of the fence, even when Marina called to her. Friends who were watching tried to encourage the filly, but Ruby refused to leave the familiar surroundings—even though her mother and Marina were waiting for her. Something had to be done, and Marina knew what it was.

It was time for a lead rope. If Ruby wouldn't move out on her own, Marina had to help her.

A lead rope is attached to the halter, in much the same way as a leash is attached to a collar. The horse feels not only the tug on the halter but also the pressure exerted by the pull on the rope, which is a message to move in that specific direction.

After gently slipping the halter on Ruby's head, Marina secured a soft lead rope and let her smell it, assuring her that it was all right. Ruby remained suspicious.

It took a great deal of time and patience to convince her that this new game was worthwhile.

Tugging a little on the rope and pulling Ruby until she moved her head in that direction, Marina then rewarded her with hugs and strokes. When she was no longer afraid, the filly began to move her body in the direction of the rope, responding to the signal. She was rewarded again.

But Ruby still refused to leave the corral. One day Marina decided to use a tail rope, which would make leading easier. The long soft rope was tied around Ruby's hindquarters and up around her neck in a non-slip loop, with the line kept a little slack. When she pulled back, she felt the pressure of the rope on her body and automatically moved forward, correctly, to relieve it. The rope was tied with a loose knot which could be untied instantly if necessary.

Using the tail rope, Marina walked Ruby around the corral, teaching her spoken commands, stopping and starting. Whenever Ruby balked, Marina gave the rope a little jerk. Whenever she moved properly, Marina rewarded her immediately. They worked together in this way until Ruby had learned to follow—to follow Trixie as well as Marina. The time had come; they could go out on the trail.

Riding out of the corral and under the cypress trees in the autumn afternoon, with her foal trailing behind, Marina knew that a whole world was waiting for Ruby's discovery...fields and forests, mountains and sea.

The first real adventure had begun.

"Birth is the most fantastic experience! I couldn't believe that she was finally here, alive and well. It was a miracle. I was afraid she would vanish at my touch. But she didn't—she was here. I stroked her forehead and she returned the greeting by nuzzling my hand. She was so soft."

"I hesitated again, not sure of what to do. I had been waiting so long for this moment. She was calm, unafraid. I put my hands on her, looking her over in minute detail. She was beautiful."

"She started to move around on her own, looking for food. I followed her, not wanting any movement of hers to escape me. Not wanting to frighten her, I went slowly. She didn't seem to mind—in fact, she showed interest. Her drink seemed to satisfy her and she was ready to move around again."

"I had her confidence, so I tried control. She seemed to accept my first effort at training. She also seemed to accept my love."

When the foal begins to move around alone, it is good to touch it firmly but very gently. Cradle the chest and speak softly to teach the foal that it is safe to be held. This is the first restraint, and an important step.

"Now came a bribe of food. She started getting cagey, remaining just out of reach, and the training turned into a game of tag. But I caught her, and rewarded her. It was important to show that she not only got food, but also love and affection. It almost always worked."

Haltering is begun as soon as possible, while the foal is small enough to handle comfortably. It's a good idea to use a handful of food for enticement and reward. Try to work in a corner to make it harder for the foal to escape you. Stand behind the rump and use your knee to hold the back leg as you slip the halter over the muzzle.

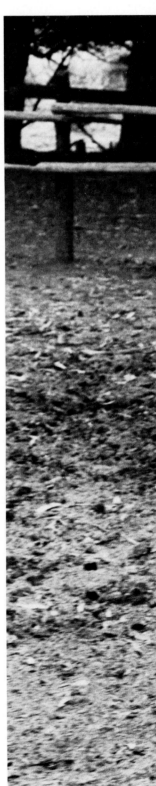

"Ruby got excited at times. She changed moods swiftly and I had to keep a watch on her all the time."

Once the foal is familiar with the halter, try leading. If the foal balks, try cradling and holding until it calms down. Keep a firm hold on the halter and a firm hand on the rump.

"It was great to get back on Trixie after such a long time. I had forgotten how important riding was. It made me think of how long I'd have to wait until I could ride Ruby. Two years can be endless."

As soon as possible, ride the dam while the foal is nearby. The foal will follow instinctively. This is the first step toward taking them out on the trail together.

Once the horses are familiar with your riding the mare while the foal follows, you can leave the paddock for the world outside the fence. Ride just beyond the gate, leave it open, and wait. Call to the foal, encourage it to follow you. Sometimes it takes more than one attempt.

"Ruby was as stubborn as her mother, at times. Coaxing was not going to make her change her mind. It got incredibly frustrating."

When a foal refuses to budge, it is possible to move it by using a tail rope, or "butt rope." Take a long, soft rope, loop it around the foal's hindquarters and up around the neck. Keep the line a little slack, tied with a non-slip loose knot. When the foal pulls back from your steady hold on the rope, the pressure it feels will make it move forward. When it responds correctly, reward it immediately.

"*I was used to the whole idea of worming, but it was a totally new experience for Ruby. She was apprehensive and this made me nervous, so I let Dr. Sharpnack take over while I watched. I just hoped that she wouldn't fight it too much.*"

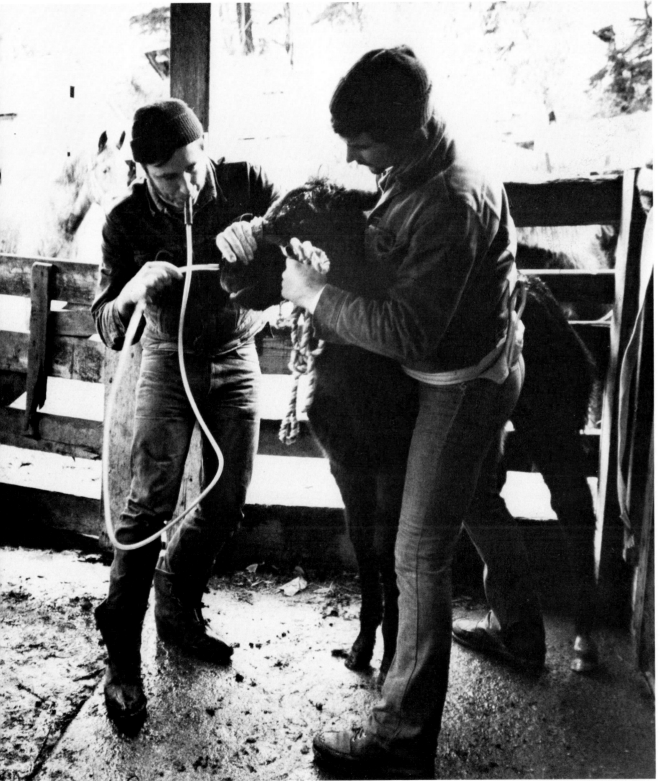

"We needed just a little more practice before I could test Ruby's trust in me. Then the turning point came: she had confidence in me. I felt ready to take her out of her familiar pasture to introduce her, unconfined, to her world. This would show the faith we had in each other."

The Young Horse

The daily care of the horses was a fixed routine. Having a paddock and a pasture, they were well protected from the elements and had a good place to exercise.

They were fed in the paddock, which had a supply of water piped in from a spring on the hill above the corral. It was available all the time in a large old enameled sink in the corner of their paddock. Watering was no problem, but it was necessary to keep the water fresh and the container clean.

Horses have small stomachs for their size and must eat twice daily. A rigid schedule is not essential as long as they eat well when they are hungriest, early in the day and in the evening. Ruby and Trixie were allowed to graze; they also ate alfalfa and hay, as well as the grain mixture which Marina took out to them as a supplement. The mixture was a combination of oats, cracked corn, and molasses, with added vitamins and minerals. There are set formulas for the amount of grain to feed horses, according to weight, activity, and climate. Nursing mares and foals usually eat more than the averages indicate.

Grooming is a time-consuming but necessary task for horse owners. Marina knew that horses in training, like Ruby, should be groomed daily, before and after trail rides or working. The most crucial part of grooming was picking out Ruby's feet, to make sure there were no stones or other foreign objects embedded in the grooves of her hooves. Such things can cripple a horse.

The first step was a thorough inspection of Ruby's feet, checking for any swelling or cuts. When picking out the hooves, Marina worked from the heel toward the toe, using a tool which had been recommended to her by the farrier—an ordinary screwdriver with dulled edges.

To Ruby, grooming was a pleasurable experience. After the filly had cooled down from her work or ride, Marina would brush Ruby as vigorously as possible (young horses have tender skin and must be treated gently).

Using a flexible rubber currycomb in one hand and a stiff brush in the other, she alternated circular strokes over her horse's coat, starting behind the ears and moving back to the tail, then brushing the belly and upper legs. The mane was cared for with a special comb. She brushed out the tail, working from the bottom up to remove snarls, and then worked on her face and lower legs with a soft brush. This same tool was used for an overall brushing at the end to make the coat shine.

Marina used a metal currycomb only when Ruby's winter coat became matted with patches of dried mud, and then she used it very lightly to remove the caked dirt.

Ruby was too young for horseshoes, and even Trixie didn't need them because of the environment in which she lived. Horses who ride only on trails and in rings, away from hard paved sur-

faces, do not need shoes. It *is* necessary, however, to keep their feet properly trimmed, so the farrier was a frequent visitor to the ranch.

Ruby was well behaved during his visits, accustomed to having her feet lifted from the very beginning of her life. She was equally at ease with the vet, who made periodic calls when shots or wormings were scheduled.

As Ruby grew stronger and more cooperative, Marina was able to begin more serious work with her. The vet gave the go-ahead for a schedule of preparation for the time when she would be ridden.

First came the saddle pad—a soft, light one. It was the first thing Ruby had ever felt on her back, and she was skeptical at first. She stood still while Marina cinched it, even though she had never experienced physical constraint around her mid-section. Marina was every excited. It was the first step in familiarizing her horse with a girth.

The next step was longeing, an excellent method of exercising a horse and a great aid in training. Before the horse is old enough to be ridden, a trainer can use longeing sessions to teach commands while controlling the horse's actions. As its musculature develops the horse can learn different gaits, and consistent work will keep the animal from developing bad habits. A horse who has had this experience before riding has a head start: longeing provides mental as well as physical training.

Using a longeing whip and a longe line, the trainer can work the horse in a circular path, cracking the whip while issuing commands. The whip is not meant for striking the horse, though the trainer might *flick* the horse with the lash—always below the hocks, not on the rump. It is used for emphasis, not punishment.

When Marina started longeing Ruby, she knew that a regular halter would be totally unsatisfactory. It fits too loosely and can slip, with the possibility of injury to the horse's eyes from the metal buckles. She used a flat nylon halter with a tight fit, one that would not slip when she was working.

Longeing is hard work. There were times when Marina felt frustrated, tired, exasperated, and plain angry. But for every difficult session, there were moments of glory when the filly responded correctly and Marina was enormously proud of her—and of herself.

It was essential to keep the lessons short and varied. Young horses, even those who have plenty of room for exercise, have a lot of nervous energy. They tend to run fast and go at it too hard. Marina made sure that Ruby had times to relax and she tried to keep the routine from becoming static.

She let Ruby know, in no uncertain terms, when she did things the right way, rewarding her immediately with affection and praise.

They worked at first in the pasture at the ranch, but they had access to a ring as well. When Marina hit a particularly rough period with Ruby,

who had started getting bored and uncooperative, Marina called on her friend Carrie, a knowledgeable horsewoman and a prize-winning rider. It helped to have an extra pair of hands around, and extra-watchful eyes for spotting difficulties before they grew into major problems.

Marina had trouble exerting enough physical control at her end of the longe line, so Carrie worked on the other side of the filly, using a lead rope to help direct her and keep her on the right track.

Marina knew that Ruby had learned what to do. The problem lay in getting her to do it without balking or fooling around. With Carrie reinforcing the oral commands Ruby developed more quickly.

Each time they started a session, they started with something which Ruby knew how to do well. New things were taught at the end of the lesson.

Horses never forget what they learn—both good habits and bad—and Marina knew that it was up to her to notice what went wrong and then deal with whatever problems appeared. It meant a lot of slow, hard work during the longeing sessions.

But Ruby learned to move smoothly in a circle without stopping, following the commands from the two trainers.

The ranch where the horses were stabled was in the rolling foothills, right on the coast. Marina liked to take her horses to the beach. Trixie had always lived near the ocean and she loved the surf; this love seemed to have passed on to Ruby. Marina let them prance and roll in the water like huge, playful puppies.

The beach was a good place for longeing Ruby. The sand was clean and free from stones. When they finished, Marina rewarded her by letting her munch the rich green grass that grew in the pasture nearby.

The landscape changed dramatically with the seasons, and Marina experienced all of them, riding Trixie with Ruby following along.

In the summer the air was hot and dry, filled with the cries of red-tailed hawks wheeling in the cloudless sky. The grass on the hills dried to a burnished gold color, and sunsets flamed over the water.

In late fall, when the rainy season began, the hills grew green again while the leaves of the deciduous trees took color. Monarch butterflies were everywhere, coming for a winter stay.

Winter brought heavy fog and violent rainstorms to the coast, but there were many days when it was clear and sunny. A ride to the beach might hold the reward of sighting whales migrating to the warm waters of Mexico, where their babies would be born.

In spring, Marina and her horses would pass through tunnels of trees pale green with new leaves, a carpet of blue forget-me-nots underfoot. The streams were full, and the horses liked to stop to play in the water.

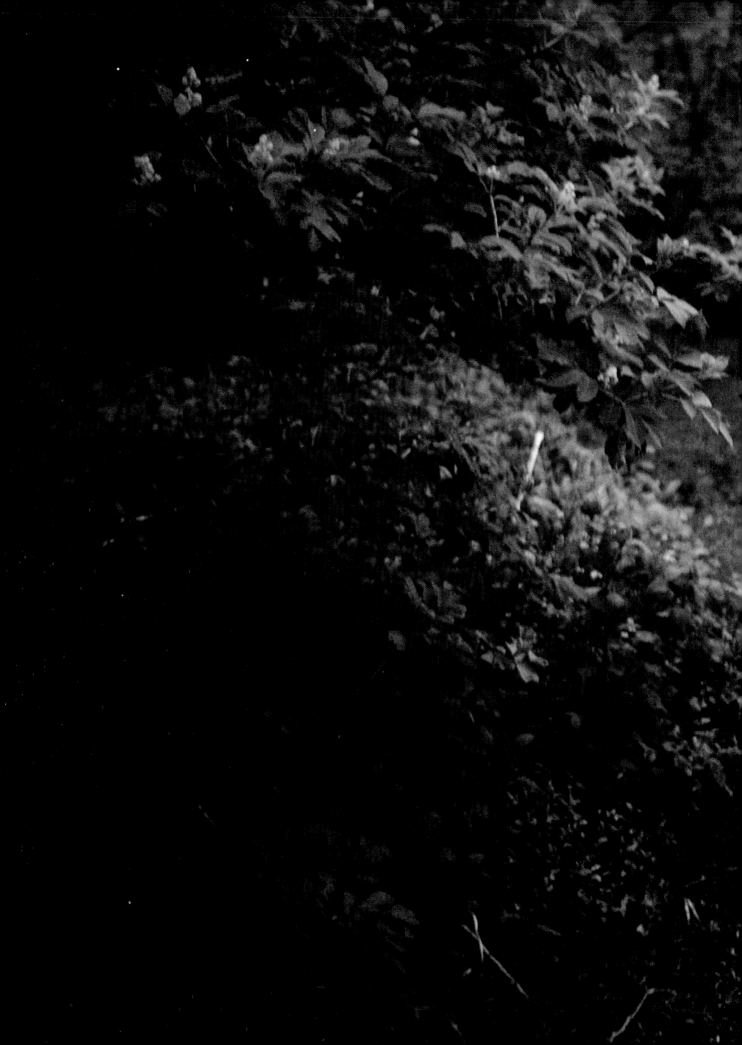

Use a light, soft saddle pad. This is the first girth your horse will feel. Allow the horse to smell the pad before you put it on. Cinch it gently, but firmly. Use the saddle pad each time you take a trail ride so the horse can become accustomed to it.

"Ruby was apprehensive about the saddle pad. I always wonder what things smell like to a horse. Can a pad smell dangerous? Fortunately there was enough trust between us to overcome her fears."

Longeing is an excellent method of exercising a horse and a great aid in training. As the foal's muscles develop, you can use the sessions for teaching it different gaits. Using a longeing whip and a longe line, work the horse in a circular path, cracking the whip while issuing commands. Never strike the horse with the whip: its sound is used for emphasis.

"Longeing. The physical action seems so simple, so elementary. Ruby did not seem to think so. I didn't mind at first, but then I realized that she knew what she should be doing. When she felt like stopping, she would. She would stare at me with a look of sheer boredom."

"The end of each day was very tiring. But I had to finish on a note of hope and confidence for the next session. It takes patience. Patience and great love."

Longeing sessions must be kept short. The training techniques must be varied to prevent a young, energetic horse from going too hard, too fast. Allow your horse time to relax and keep the routine from becoming boring to either of you. After your horse has performed well, reward it immediately with affection and kind words.

"It was so satisfying when Ruby did what I asked. All the work seemed worth it when I saw her do a lesson correctly."

"Ruby was getting stronger every day. It was getting harder and harder to control her. It was frightening to know that she could just take off, dragging me behind."

"It was much easier when my friend Carrie helped out. Four strong arms are better than two, and it was good to have someone there for support."

It is a good idea to have another person who can help control your horse when longeing becomes rougher. When your friend works with a lead rope on the other side of the horse, the horse can be directed more easily and you can exert enough control on the longe line to keep your horse on the right track. Your friend can also help to spot the problems you might miss when you're too involved with the longeing.

"She still got rambunctious at times. I often felt very angry with her. It was so frustrating: she knew what to do, but she just wouldn't perform."

There are times when longeing becomes a contest of strength and will between you and your horse. Things seem to go every way but right. It is good to stop then, to remember other times when you worked together well. Relax and try to develop your patience. Teaching has its ups and downs, its pleasures and its difficulties.

"Anger...frustration...desperation—I felt all these so many times. I doubted my sanity for keeping such stubborn, selfish, impossible animals."

Start each longeing session with something your horse knows well, then teach new things at the end. When problems appear, work on them right away so that your horse does not develop bad habits. Eventually, the horse will be moving smoothly in a circle, following your commands, performing correctly. Grazing in rich grass is a good reward for work well done.

"All my feelings of frustration were repaid when Ruby cooperated. It was such an accomplishment when she did what I asked!"

Have the horse's feet
trimmed frequently to keep
them in good condition.
When the farrier works, he
examines the feet carefully
before picking them out.
Then he cleans the soles
with his farrier's knife and
trims away any dead horn
which might interfere with
the rest of the hoof. He
takes a rasp and smooths
the edges of the hoof, re-
moving any part which
might chip or break.

Growing Towards Freedom

As Ruby's second birthday approached, a new training program began. There was a gradual introduction to the equipment which would be used in riding—the bridle and the saddle. Marina presented them to Ruby in the same unhurried way in which she had accustomed her to the saddle pad.

She had mixed feelings about bridling Ruby for the first time. She loved watching her horse run free and she got a great deal of pleasure out of leading her and working with her. The bridle would be a stronger control and a big leap forward in her growing up. Marina was afraid Ruby would feel the bit in her mouth as a betrayal of all the gentleness she had experienced in the work that had been done up to this point.

She was also apprehensive about the physical aspects of the first bridling. Even though Marina had bridled horses for years, she had never seen anyone put a bit in a young horse's mouth for the very first time. Would Ruby accept it willingly or refuse it?

Marina remembered that when she first got Trixie—a seasoned horse—she had been forced to bribe her with carrots to get her mouth open for the bit!

There was a small feeling of sadness, too, at the realization that Ruby was no longer a foal, a baby. This was a rite of passage for both of them.

The bridle she planned to use had a rubber snaffle; it was firm, but soft enough for Ruby's tender mouth. Marina approached Ruby calmly, allowing her to smell it. She didn't tie the horse, as she wanted Ruby to be relaxed; besides, there was hay nearby to capture the filly's attention.

Standing in position to the left of her horse, Marina held the bridle and brought the bit into place, close to Ruby's mouth. She stuck her thumb into the very back of Ruby's lips, forcing her to open her mouth. This was an unexpected touch and Ruby pulled back, but the force of Marina's thumb on the gum—where there are no teeth—made her open her jaw. Immediately, Marina directed the bit between Ruby's teeth and over her tongue, simultaneously pulling the bridle up across her nose and putting the bit into place. She held it there with a steady pressure while she gently slipped the headstall over Ruby's ears, one at a time.

Ruby's reaction was surprise rather than fear. She moved her mouth around the bit, tasting it and rolling her tongue over it, but she didn't spook.

Marina adjusted the height of the bit to create just the right amount of tension, and the job was done. She was thrilled. Her horse had accepted the bit with no trouble at all!

When Ruby was bridled, Marina walked her around the corral, leading her to get her used to the control on her mouth.

After that first successful session, Marina

worked with her daily, increasing the amount of time spent with the bit until she felt that Ruby was totally accustomed to the bridle.

In preparation for saddling Ruby, Marina had been practicing what she called "weight training." Ruby's back strengthened as she grew; Marina started leaning against her, stretching out over her back, gradually letting more of her own weight rest on her. Though it was too soon to sit on her or to put her entire weight on Ruby's back, Marina made sure the filly adjusted gradually to the contact and the extra load.

The day came when it was time to saddle up. As she went up the hill to lead Ruby from the pasture, Marina felt anxious about Ruby's reaction to the new bulk and weight on her back.

She decided not to tie Ruby. A few days before her horse had been frightened while tied, when a gate had swung open and a gelding had run toward her. If Ruby became agitated, Marina could simply grab the halter to restrain her.

She knew that she had a docile horse, but she also knew that there is always a chance that any horse will become enraged and try to buck the saddle off when it is fastened for the first time.

Trixie's Western pony saddle was light enough for Ruby. Marina brought it to her and allowed her to smell it before she began.

A thick saddle pad is especially important when a saddle is placed on a green horse, to protect the tender skin. Marina put the pad on a little forward and slid it back into place, to make sure that the hair underneath would not be irritated by being pushed the wrong way.

She lifted the saddle very gently into position, well over the withers so that it would not slide from side to side. The cinching was done gently and very gradually. Ruby stood still, more inter-

Basic Guide to Health Care for Foal from Birth to Two Years

At birth
1. Basic physical exam by veterinarian for any health problems.
2. Long-lasting antibiotic injection.
3. Tetanus antitoxin if mare is not on a regular program.
4. Antiseptic application to stump of umbilical cord.
5. Enema, if there is any problem passing fetal stool.

2 months
1. First systemic use of medication to remove bloodworms and round worms. This can be done by owner with some of the newer paste wormers. The important thing is that this should be repeated every two months until the age of one year. After that age the worming may be decreased to

ested in the nearby food than in the operation taking place.

The saddle was cinched snugly against her belly, but Marina left it loose enough on the sides for Marina to insert two fingers between the rope cinch and the flesh. When she had finished, she tied the stirrups together underneath with a soft rope to keep them from bumping against Ruby when she moved.

At first, she *didn't* move. She glanced back over her shoulder, sniffing suspiciously at the saddle.

Marina was delighted when she led Ruby around the corral. She hadn't spooked, and despite the unfamiliar weight and pressure of the

---

four times yearly.
2. A farrier should examine the foal's feet and begin trimming program.

4 months
1. First of tetanus toxoid series, to be repeated in 4-6 weeks.
2. Routine worming.
3. Rhinopneumonitis vaccination, to be repeated in 4-6 weeks.
4. Western and Eastern sleeping sickness vaccination.

$4\frac{1}{2}$ months
1. Second sleeping sickness vaccination.

5 months
1. Second tetanus toxoid, rhinopneumonitis vaccinations.

6 months
1. Routine worming.

8 months
1. Routine worming.

10 months
1. Routine worming.

12 months
1. Routine worming.

15 months
1. Routine worming.
2. Animal vaccines for tetanus, rhinopneumonitis and sleeping sickness.

18 months
1. Routine worming.

21 months
1. Routine worming.

24 months
1. Routine worming.

saddle causing a change in her balance, she moved easily and willingly. She looked like a real horse now!

When Ruby was content to move freely about the corral with the saddle on, Marina took her out on the trail. She followed Trixie, learning to adjust to the shifting load and the extra pounds.

They followed the easy trails, the fire roads which were unpaved and clear, going from the ranch to the ring. The rides were kept short at first, then increased in length as Ruby's stamina increased. Marina used the saddle for further training. It was too early to swing over with all her weight, but she could place her foot in the left stirrup, gradually adding more pressure, familiarizing Ruby with the change in balance which occurs when a rider mounts.

Longeing with the saddle was more demanding. It took time for Ruby to feel comfortable enough to get back to work, but Marina per-

---

Suggested Reading

Ball, Charles E., Saddle Up!, the Farm Journal Book of Western Horsemanship *(Philadelphia and New York: J. B. Lippincott Company, 1970)*
A guide to buying, training and showing a horse.

Coggins, Jack, The Horseman's Bible *(New York: Doubleday and Company, 1966)*
A basic guide plus a concise history of breeds.

Marlin, Herb, & Savitt, Sam, How To Take Care of Your Horse Until the Vet Comes *(New York: Dodd, Mead & Company, 1975)*
A horse health and first-aid guide.

Ulmer, Donald E., & Jurgenson, Elwood M., Approved Practices in Raising and Handling Horses *(Illinois: The Interstate Printers & Publishers, Inc., 1974)*
Comprehensive list of activities which involve approved practices, with information on how they should be done.

Young, John Richard, Schooling for Young Riders *(Norman, Oklahoma: University of Oklahoma Press, 1970)*
A true, subjective account of the selection, breaking and schooling of one horse and the training of his young rider. A commonsense guide.

severed. She knew that the effort was necessary to prepare Ruby for riding.

It was essential to keep Ruby working without boredom until she had learned to respond perfectly. She was independent, and Marina had to prove her own power by sticking with her.

Sometimes the sessions went beautifully; the filly performed like a professional. Then the next day she would act like a balky novice.

Marina watched her carefully, knowing that Ruby *was* learning, however erratically. She knew what to do and was capable of doing it. Marina got tougher and Ruby seemed to realize that, in their sessions at least, it was time for serious business.

Until Ruby obeyed her spoken commands, there would be no riding for Marina. She had waited a long time.

Finally, things began to look brighter. Marina spent a lot more time in the ring, longeing Ruby. She rewarded her consistently and tried all the tricks she knew to get her to the necessary level of training.

The work and fatigue and frustration drifted into memory when Marina saw before her a filly prepared for the next, the biggest adventure: her first ride.

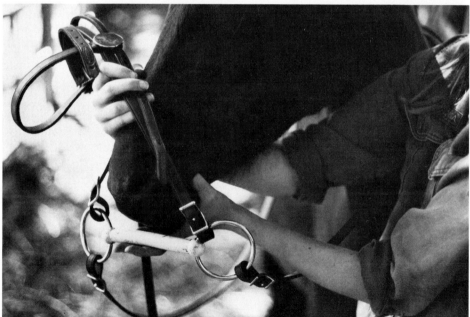

Bridling your horse: stand on the left side of the horse. Put your right hand around the horse's nose, holding the headstall. The reins should be up on the horse's neck. Rest the bit on the fingers of your left hand and bring it close to the horse's lips. Stick the thumb of your left hand into the very corner of the horse's mouth, where there are no teeth. Put pressure on the gum until the horse opens its mouth.

"I was worried when the time came to bridle Ruby. I had never seen anyone put a bit into a horse's mouth for the very first time, and I wasn't sure how she would react. Even though I used a rubber bit, I thought that she would feel it was a betrayal—it wouldn't be like all the gentle things I had done before. This would be an important act of control over her."

Once the mouth is open, direct the bit between the teeth and over the tongue, while pulling the bridle with your right hand across the face to bring the bit into place. When the bit is in the horse's mouth, hold it in place by keeping your right hand steady on the bridle. Move your left hand up to the left side of the headstall, slip it over the ears very gently (first left side, then right). Bring the forelock over the head band. Adjust the height of the bit by pulling it snug so that the bit makes little wrinkles in the corner of the horse's mouth. Voila!

To remove the bridle, slip the headstall over the ears. Make sure the bit is still in the horse's mouth, which must be wide open before you try to remove the bit. That way you will not hit the teeth.

"I was happy that the bridling went so well, yet I felt a little sad when I realized that Ruby was no longer a foal."

"*I kept putting weight on Ruby's back by leaning across it. This got her used to the idea that I would be sitting on her, as I sat on her mother. That time was drawing near.*"

"Ruby accepted the saddle with her usual trust—and curiosity. It made her look grown-up and it was very moving to see my filly looking so horsey. I felt that all my work was beginning to pay off."

After your vet has made sure your horse's muscles are sufficiently developed, you can saddle it for the first time. Tie your horse if you expect any spooking. Allow it to smell the saddle before you begin. Be sure that the saddle pad is thick enough to protect the horse's tender skin and that the hair is smooth underneath the pad. Lift the saddle into position very gently, well over the withers, so that it doesn't slide. Cinch the saddle snugly but leave it loose enough on the sides so that two fingers can fit between the rope cinch and the horse's flesh. Tie the stirrups together underneath to keep them from bumping against the horse when it moves.

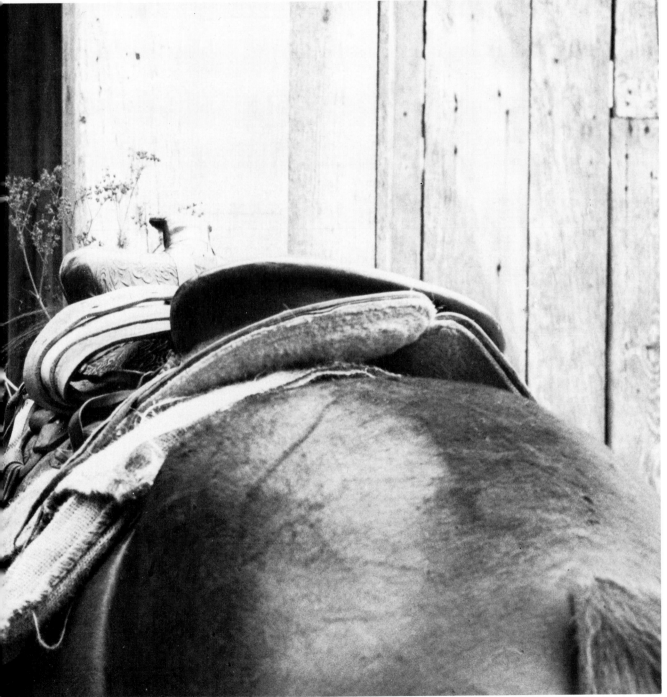

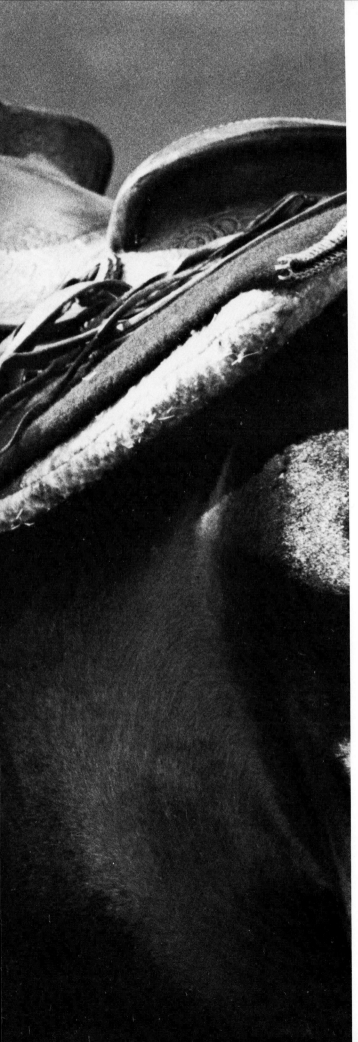

"The early work with the saddle pad served its purpose. Ruby trusted me, even though she was curious about what was on her back."

"I kept testing her, seeing how much she would do for me, especially with the new weight of the saddle. I loved it when she really worked!"

"Ruby was so patient and accepting. I was getting closer and closer to the point of riding her. The momentum was gathering inside me."

When your horse is used to the saddle, you can begin adding your own weight gradually. Jump up lightly, with your hands on the horn and the cantle for balance, remaining for a few seconds at a time. In this way the horse feels uneven weight and it will be natural when you finally get into the saddle.

"There were just a few more things to do. Ruby was working well. I was getting nervous: I had been waiting a long time and the reality was almost at hand. I still had my doubts, not only about her, but also about myself. As the time for riding came closer I wondered if we were really ready for that big step."

The First Ride: A Real Beginning

The long-awaited day came at last. It was a day very much like the morning when Marina had first seen the tiny foal beside her mother in the corral. There was fog in the cool air, with intermittent breakthroughs of autumn sunshine.

Marina had been nervous before with Ruby, but that feeling had been nothing compared to the way she felt on what she thought of as "the day of judgment." Everything she had taught Ruby, all the work and planning and concentration, would be tested in the single experience of the first ride.

There is no way of knowing in advance how a horse will react to it. Although the vet had checked Ruby's size and weight, Marina was concerned about whether her muscles were strong enough to hold up. She knew that there was always the chance that Ruby would spook, that either of them could be injured.

As she and Carrie sat at the ranch talking over their plans for the ride, Marina had butterflies in her stomach. It was worse than stagefright. This ride was to be the proof that all she had done with Ruby had paid off.

From the ranch they took the trail to the ring, under the cypress trees and over the fire road. The ring was a familiar place and Ruby was content to graze near her mother while Carrie and Marina talked.

Carrie warned Marina to be very cautious and slow in her actions, to be prepared for anything, to expect the unexpected. She would be there if she were needed, but the control had to come from Marina.

They saddled Ruby, using Carrie's light English saddle over a Western saddle pad which offered extra protection. Carrie attached the line to the halter.

The moment had arrived. Marina's heart pounded and questions raced through her mind. Was the time right? Was Ruby ready? Was *she* ready? It was a moment of terror mixed with delight.

Carrie stood near Ruby, holding the emergency line. She was there to help, to keep Ruby calm.

Marina mounted very, very slowly, swinging her leg over and coming down as lightly as possible. On the other side of the saddle, Carrie held the stirrup down to balance the weight as Marina mounted. It was done so gradually that Marina felt she was in a slow-motion film.

Ruby remained calm as Marina mounted, but when they first moved forward, she seemed con-fused—her balance was affected by the new weight on her back, and she was unsteady on her feet. Carrie held the line and walked beside them. Marina directed Ruby with the lightest possible leg pressure, using a forward movement of her pelvis and giving Ruby the spoken commands she had taught her. Marina managed to keep her legs relaxed but firm, though she felt like trembling with excitement.

This was like her first ride on a roller coaster, or the first time she had caught a big wave, body-surfing. She was just as thrilled, just as nervous.

She rode Ruby only halfway around the ring, at a walk. Time seemed to freeze for Marina. Aware of the tiniest movement of the horse beneath her, she was all but holding her breath as they progressed on their small journey.

Suddenly Ruby stopped in her tracks. Marina reached out and stroked her, encouraging her to move on, and Carrie tugged gently on the line. Again, they moved forward.

It was all right, after all. Marina swallowed hard, trying to remain relaxed.

Both Marina and Carrie constantly watched Ruby's movements, checking her balance and her footing. Though she was still unsure in her new role, she was docile and offered no further resistance.

They had gone far enough for one day. Marina didn't want to push Ruby too hard. It was important not to tire her or demand too much.

She checked the reins gently to stop. When she dismounted, as slowly and carefully as she had mounted, Carrie held the stirrup again on the opposite side to counterbalance.

Marina was ecstatic! She felt shaky, still, as Carrie congratulated her, but it was over, at last. She had a horse, a *real horse!*

If there had ever been a time for celebration, this was it! All the hours and days and months of work had led them to this place where a simple ride took on the magic and glow of a miracle. She hugged Ruby and she hugged Carrie and she felt like hugging herself. For Marina, it was the beginning of a whole new life with Ruby, who had proved herself that afternoon.

After the initial ride it was time to start building up Ruby's confidence. Her legs grew stronger and her muscles continued to develop. Marina rode her every day. For safety's sake she always had another person in the ring—Ruby's behavior was still unpredictable. At first someone would hold the emergency line; eventually Marina rode without it, but someone was always nearby.

The first ring training taught Ruby to move in a straight line at different gaits, to stop and to turn. The cues Marina used were very gentle and subtle. It was important to sit loosely enough to follow the horse's movement, keeping her center of gravity vertically above Ruby's. As Ruby's movements shifted her center, Marina coordinated, going with her. In this way, Marina *felt* the horse, and the horse became used to her.

The less a rider uses her hands for influence, the more influence the legs will develop. Marina used the reins without forceful action, concentrating on the pressure from her legs to guide Ruby through her movements. She changed gaits frequently to get the feel of riding her.

Once Ruby proved to be capable in the work they did in the ring, Marina knew that she could take her on the trail without Trixie for the first time. Again, Carrie was there to help, walking beside them with an emergency line.

They went from the ranch to the path through the woods, a ride they had made many times during the two years of training. But Ruby was suspicious; it was different without Trixie. She glanced at the trees and bushes and when she heard a noise in the underbrush ahead of her, she reared.

Carrie was right there, holding the line taut, and she rushed forward to grab Ruby's halter. Remembering her early training, Marina instinctively pulled her feet from the stirrups, prepared to vault if necessary. She pushed off, safely, as Ruby fell.

It was a frightening moment, but they calmed Ruby. After checking to see that she was all right they relaxed. Marina knew that she had to get right back on her horse, to prove that there was no change between them as a result of the incident. Ruby had to learn that bolting and rearing would get her nowhere.

The importance of the situation was not lost on Marina. It was the first time she had felt in danger with Ruby. She had to take things more seriously, to watch out for both of them from then on.

That meant working with her on easier trails—flat, clear paths with no trees, where no birds or animals would be likely to startle her.

So she used the meadows, golden brown at that time of the year. Thistles and weeds bent in the wind, and the tall grass parted as they moved through it.

Marina guided Ruby through that landscape slowly and carefully, staying on paths which were free of obstacles. Ruby became familiar with them and learned to like the ride, gradually becoming more content in her role.

They had come a long way together since the August morning when Ruby was born. Marina had thought that the birth of the foal was the beginning. Now she knew that their first ride had actually been the beginning of the time when they would be on their own, independent and free.

One afternoon she remembered something written by C.S. Lewis. When she went home, she copied it down:

"But for them it was only the beginning of the real story. All their life in this world and all their adventures...had only been the cover and the title page: now at last they were beginning Chapter One of the great story, which no one on earth has ever read, which goes on forever, in which every chapter is better than the one before."*

The little girl's dream had come true. There they were, the young woman and her horse, riding freely over the hills and through the forests, through the meadows to the sea.

*Lewis, C.S., *The Last Battle*. London: Collier Books, 1970

"This was the day of reckoning, which would decide whether all the love I had given to Ruby would pay off. The energy, excitement, and fear grew to an almost unbearable point."

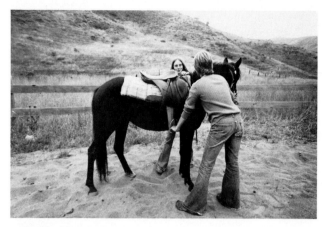

"By the actual time of mounting, I was a wreck. Ruby seemed so skinny! I was used to a fat mare, but there I was, sitting on her narrow back, on my horse!"

It is essential to have another person with you when you mount your horse for the first time. A lead rope can work as an emergency line for controlling and directing the horse, if necessary. Your friend should hold the stirrup down on the other side to balance the weight as you mount. Do this very, very slowly, swinging your leg over and coming down as lightly as possible. Be aware of your horse's mood.

"We walked around very slowly. Her legs were weak, I could feel that. But she was great! Every difference in movement brought a new shot of fear to me."

The horse will be nervous and its balance will be affected by this new weight, so you must proceed very carefully, keeping your legs relaxed but firm. Your friend should walk beside you, still holding the lead rope. Remember to use the commands you have taught your horse and direct it as gently as possible. It is important not to demand too much the first day.

"When I got off, I was re-
lieved—ecstatic. I had been
waiting over two years for
this moment. Carrie said,
'Marina, you've got yourself a
horse!' She was right. She
was a beautiful *horse!*"

"Once Ruby was used to my weight, I tried her without an emergency line. She did well, but her legs were still weak. It worried me when she faltered. I worked to strengthen her for the next giant step: taking her outside the fences."

Work on developing the strength in your horse's legs, teaching it to move in a straight line at different gaits, to stop and to turn. Remember to sit loosely, to *feel* the horse. Change gaits frequently and use the reins lightly; depend more on the gentle pressure from your legs to guide the horse. Young horses are unpredictable and it is essential to have someone else standing by at this stage of training, in case of an emergency.

"Out on the trail Ruby was jumpier than I'd expected her to be. When she heard a noise in the brush, she bolted. I first thought of how to stop her, but when she started to fall, I got away from her as quickly as possible, by vaulting. I was badly shaken, and so was Ruby. But scared though I was, I knew I had to get right back on. I was glad Carrie was there, that I wasn't alone, when it happened."

139

"I did a lot of review work with Ruby in the ring after that trail ride. She did extremely well, and I decided it was time for us to be out on our own, without an emergency line. This was a great experience of freedom. It was beautiful to ride the horse I had raised, out into the wilds. It was time to explore our world, two animals of different species, cooperating through love."

The Black Filly

The black filly gallops at night,
And favors her mother at dawn.
Her hoofbeat's like thunder
And her whinny like a child's cry.
—MARINA FUSCO at age 8, 1969